Everything the Internet
didn't teach you about
Knitting

by Rita Weiss

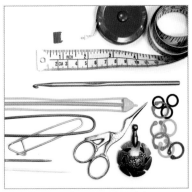

complete tool guide

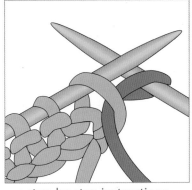

step-by-step instructions

learning about gauge

plus easy beginner projects

Leisure Arts, Inc.
Maumelle, Arkansas

Produced by

Production Team

Creative Directors: Jean Leinhauser and Rita Weiss

Senior Technical Editor: Ellen W. Liberles

Photographer: Carol Wilson Mansfield

Book Design: Linda Causee

Diagrams ©2013 by The Creative Partners™ LLC.
Reproduced by special permission.

We have made every effort to ensure that these instructions are accurate and complete. We cannot, however, be responsible for human error, typographical mistakes, or variations in individual work.

Library of Congress Control Number: 2012955665

ISBN-13: 978-1-4647-0740-7

Introduction

This book is for my friend, Barb. . . because she asked.

My friend Barb is one smart lady. In addition to being a mother to four wonderful children and a medical doctor, she can give you an immediate answer to any question you might ask by consulting her computer or smart phone with ease and aplomb.

So when I saw Barb knitting a scarf, I was not amazed. I just assumed that Barb knew how to knit. But, when she started to ask me some very elementary questions, I became confused. "Didn't you learn that when you learned to knit," I asked. "Who taught you without showing you that?"

"I taught myself," Barb responded. "I learned from a web site on the Internet."

That's when it occurred to me that, like Barb, there are lots of knitters out there who were able to teach themselves to knit by following a YouTube presentation. They've learned the basic stitches, but they haven't learned about the various types of knitting needles. No one has taught them about the different kinds of yarn and how to tell one from another. They've never learned about the importance of gauge and how to make a gauge swatch. They don't know how to read a knitting pattern: what all those symbols, asterisks, daggers and brackets mean.

And, maybe most important of all, they don't know what to do when they've made a mistake.

So, we've produced this book for Barb and for all the Barbs out there who have taught themselves to knit. If you can't remember what the Internet taught you, or if you're just not knitting with the ease that other knitters around you seem to have, then turn to page 77 for our Refresher Course in Knitting. But if you just need some help in reading a yarn label or in determining whether a pattern could possibly be too difficult for you, you've come to the right place.

Here are the answers to those questions you could find no one to ask.

– Rita Weiss

Contents

Tools

One of the great advantages of deciding you want to be a knitter is the realization that you won't need a lot of tools. If you wanted to make furniture instead of just knitting sweaters, you'd need a lot of saws, hammers, nails, awls, screwdrivers and more. Knitting, however, is unusual in that it needs only two basic tools: two sticks and some string. As knitting evolved, the string became yarn and the sticks became the knitting needles we know today.

KNITTING NEEDLES

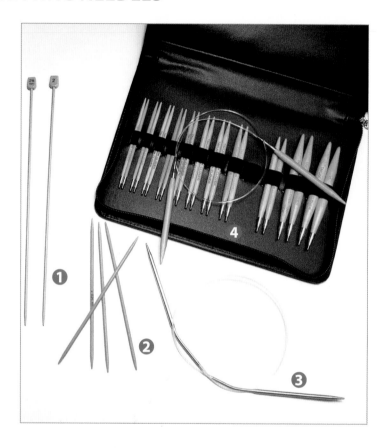

❶ Straight Needles

❷ Double-points

❸ Circular

❹ Interchangeable
   Circular Knitting Needles

Old knitting needles, often called knitting pins, knitting wires or knitting woods, were made by knitters themselves. The knitter would use whatever materials were available: wood, bone, ivory, copper, wire, walrus tusks, tortoiseshells and even iron or steel. As with modern needles, these early needles needed to have a long shaft and were tapered to a point.

To keep the point sharp enough, the knitter would grind the points when they became blunt.

Today there are basically three types of knitting needles: straight needles, double-point needles and circular needles. They are made with a variety of materials and are available in a number of sizes. Each of the needles can be used to knit, but there are certain advantages or disadvantages in using any of the needles for certain work.

Single-points or Straight Needles are the most popular and most widely recognized type of needle. They are basically two straight "sticks" with a tapered point (not as sharp as a sewing needle) at one end and at the other end a knob or cap which prevents stitches from falling off the needle. The "stick" holds the completed stitches, while the tapered point is used to form new stitches. Sold in pairs, single-points are traditionally about 10" to 14" long although single-points in shorter or longer lengths are available. These needles are used almost entirely for knitting flat two-dimensional projects where the work is done back and forth in rows. The disadvantage of using single-points, however, is apparent when attempting to knit a large fabric piece. Since the entire weight of the knitting hanging from the needle must be supported by the knitting needles, this can cause great stress to the knitter's hands, and many knitters use a circular needle for large projects.

Double-point needles: Historians regard these as the oldest needles, and they were originally used for all knitting: probably garments knitted in the round. Today double-points—often referred to as dpn—are used mainly for small objects, which have no seams, such as socks and necklines, while the circular needle is used for larger circular objects. The knitting is therefore not turned at the end of each row but worked around and around, making a spiral tube. Double-points are also often used in lace knitting when the project, such as a scarf or doily, is worked from the center out. The knitter begins the project with a set of double-points and then may graduate to a circular needle as the project gets larger.

As the name implies, double-points are made with points at both ends of the needle, which allows them to be knit from each end. They are sold today in fewer lengths than the straight or circular needles—the most popular length being 7"—but they can be found in sizes 0 to 15. Double-points are sold in sets of either 4 needles, which are most common in the US, or in sets of 5 needles, usually found in other parts of the world. One needle company offers sets of 6 in case you lose one. When working with 4 needles, the knitting is held on three needles, and the 4th needle is used to do the work; when working with 5 needles, the knitting is held on 4 needles, with the 5th needle employed to make the stitches.

While you can knit back and forth with double-points, you have to be careful that you don't drop stitches off the end not in use. By attaching a point protector to the end of a double-point needle, it can be converted to a straight needle and used for flat knitting.

Circular needles (sometimes called "twin pins") were a late addition to the knitter's tool collection. Introduced after the end of World War I, the needle consists of a length of flexible nylon cable or wire of varying lengths with two pointed needle tips at either end. It is actually the same as having two straight needles joined together. The tips can be made of metal, plastic or wood, allowing the knitter to choose her favorite.

Circular needles were developed to work in seamless rounds, creating a seamless tube as in the body of a sweater. In making a circular project, the knitting is joined as it is worked around and around; a marker is usually used to mark the start of a row or round. Many knitters, however, now prefer a circular needle for flat knitting as well, working back and forth. It is especially useful when the straight needles cannot accommodate the number of stitches in a pattern. Using a circular needle can make the knitting move faster with less fatigue for the knitter since the weight of the knitting is distributed evenly between the points of the needle. In addition, if the work is especially heavy—as in knitting a huge afghan—the work is actually sitting in the knitter's lap rather than supported by the needles. For those with arthritis, rheumatism, carpal-tunnel syndrome or sensitive hands, working with a circular needle may be preferable. When circular needles are used on flat projects, the knitting is done back and forth without joining at the end of a row.

There are other advantages to the circular needle as well. When the knitter has completed her work for the day, she can push the knitting back from the tips and onto the cable, which now acts as a stitch holder, until the next knitting session. Since the knitting is created by the use of one needle, it is virtually impossible to lose a knitting needle in the midst of a project. And finally, the knitter who knits with a circular needle takes up much less room and avoids poking a companion with a long needle.

Although circular needles are found in many lengths of cable from 12" to 60", the most popular lengths are 29" and 36". If the knitter is planning to use many different sizes of circular needles, a component knitting set for making circular needles in all sizes might be a good choice. These sets contain cables to create circular needles from 20" to 60" along with points in sizes ranging from 2 through 15. When using the circular needle for knitting in the round, it is important to remember that the circumference of the piece being knit should be at least 2" larger than the length of the entire needle.

KNITTING NEEDLE MATERIALS

Knitting needles are made in a variety of materials, each of which has advantages and disadvantages. Years ago knitting needles were made of bone, especially whale bone. These needles are no longer sold today and have become collector's items. The three main materials used today for knitting needles are: plastic, metal (including aluminum and steel), and wood (including bamboo). Today's knitter can choose the needle that fits her particular style and the project that she is working on. The kind of needle to be used is an individual choice made by the knitter. Often the choice depends upon the stitches being used and the type of yarn as well as the knitter's own special knitting habits. The perfect knitting needle will be light so that it doesn't add to the weight on the knitter's hands as well as strong enough so that it will not bend as the work progresses. The tip of the needle needs to be well tapered but not too pointy so that the stitches can be worked without splitting the yarn.

Plastic needles seem to be warm to the touch and permit the yarn to slide across the needle with ease. The needles make no noise as the knitting moves across the row. They have certain disadvantages, however, depending upon the needles you select. There is great variation in plastic needles, but many plastic needles have blunt points or points that can wear down as you knit with them. Some kinds of plastic needles tend to catch the yarn, and some knitters find that cotton yarns tend to stick.

Most of the plastic needles are lightweight and a good choice for knitters with arthritis, but some of the larger ones can be heavy, adding weight to your work.

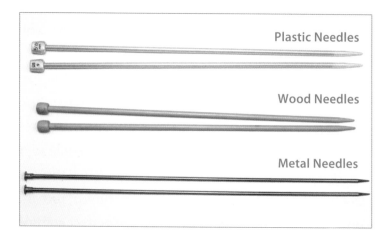

Metal needles (including aluminum, steel, nickel-plated) tend to be cool to the touch. They are great for knitters who want to knit fast as there is very little friction, thereby allowing the stitches to move rapidly across the needle. They very rarely will bend or break so they will last a long time. Some knitters, however, find them too slippery. In addition, some knitters are turned off by the clicking sound the needles make as you work. For knitters who like to knit tightly, metal needles work best, as they do when working with yarns that might stick to the needle, such as wools, alpaca or angora yarns. If, however, the yarn is a slippery one, such as silks or rayons, or if the knitter works loosely, metal needles are not a good choice. Metal needles come in many types and sizes. Aluminum needles are best if the knitter is looking for a light metal needle, or if she wishes to neutralize warm hands.

Aluminum needles are readily available in most craft stores and tend to be fairly inexpensive. Their smooth surface allows the stitches to move very quickly and with very little resistance. Brass and steel needles are smooth but can be heavy. Since many metal needles are nickel-plated, the knitter needs to be aware of any allergies to nickel. Metal tends to be unyielding, and this may prove a problem for those with arthritis, carpal-tunnel syndrome or sensitive hands.

Wood Needles (including bamboo) While bamboo is actually not a wood, it has all of the properties of wood and is classified with wood needles. When working with lace, slippery yarns or very complicated patterns, wood needles, such as bamboo, might be the best choice. Knitters who find that they perspire when knitting often prefer wood needles because these needles tend to absorb the perspiration. Wood needles can be made of birch, ebony, rosewood, or walnut. Wood needles are lightweight, feel warm in the knitter's hands and have a slightly rough surface. These needles are usually treated with a coating to keep them from wearing out. This means that the knitting process moves more slowly and precisely, but that is an advantage when working with complex patterns or when starting to learn to knit. The disadvantage of wooden needles is their tendency to break or splinter; in addition, the needles made of rarer woods can be expensive.

These needles are a great choice for beginners, as they tend to grab the yarn as you work. Experienced knitters are often turned off by wood's ability to grip the yarn, as this can slow down the work. Smaller sizes break easily, and larger sizes are heavy, adding to the weight of the project.

The type of material chosen for your needle is strictly up to the individual knitter. Choose the needle that works best for you and for the project that you are making. No one can tell you what type of needle you want. Once you have become proficient at knitting, you might want to invest in some of the exotic needles currently on the market. Many of these needles are hand crafted from magnificent woods, such as rosewood, birch or ebony. Many of these needles are quite expensive, so wait until you are certain that you want that particular size needle before you make your purchase.

Size of all knitting needles is determined by the length and the diameter of the needle, and it is important to consider both when purchasing knitting needles.

Needle Diameter The diameter of the knitting needle determines the size of the needle. For a long time there was a great deal of confusion on the numbers listed for sizes on knitting needles.

Different manufacturers often used different markings. Some used a system of letters and some used a number system. In addition there were two different methods used to size needles in the US and the UK, and some needle manufacturers included a metric equivalent. Several years ago the Craft Yarn Council, an organization of yarn manufacturers, yarn publishers and hook and needle manufacturers, agreed to make metric (millimeter/mm) sizing more prominent on packaging and to list the US sizes, both numbers and/or letters on the packaging.

In the metric system, a lower number indicates a thinner needle. In the US, the same rule applies to sizes of needles: lower numbers indicate thinner needles. Unfortunately in the UK, the sizing is the exact opposite: lower numbers indicate thicker needles. Here is a chart that shows needle sizes in both the US and the UK. Interestingly the only time when the needle sizes match is on the size 7 (4.5mm). If you still have a question about needle size, use a needle gauge (see page 18). Needles above 10mm (US Size 15) are usually called "Jiffy Needles" because the large diameter makes the work move very quickly and usually produces a very loosely woven fabric.

KNITTING NEEDLE CONVERSION CHART

Metric	US	UK
2 mm	0	14
2.25 mm	1	13
2.75 mm	2	12
3 mm	N/A	11
3.25 mm	3	10
3.50 mm	4	N/A
3.75 mm	5	9
4 mm	6	8
4.50 mm	7	7
5 mm	8	6
5.50 mm	9	5
6 mm	10	4
6.50 mm	10.5	3
7 mm	N/A	2
7.50 mm	N/A	1
8 mm	11	0
9 mm	13	00
10 mm	15	000
12.75 mm	17	N/A
15 mm	19	N/A
19 mm	35	N/A
25mm	50	N/A

Needle Length: Knitting needles are available in different lengths. The choice for which length is dependent upon the number of stitches in a project. If you have fewer stitches in your pattern, pick a shorter needle; if you have more stitches required, use a longer needle. The stitches need to fit along the needle without crowding where they might be in danger of falling off. Because very long needles can be awkward to work with (you are in danger of poking someone with the needle as you work), many knitters prefer using circular needles for large projects. Work the project as you would for flat knitting and turn the work at the end of every row.

The most popular needle lengths for straight needles are 10" (25 cm) and 14" (35 cm) , for double-points, 7" (17 cm) and for circulars 29" (73 cm).

OTHER KNITTING TOOLS

While all of these tools are not necessary for everyday knitting, it is handy to have at least some of them.

Cable Stitch Needle: This is a short needle with points at both ends (some have a hump in the middle) that is designed to hold some of the stitches while other stitches are worked. If the cable needle is held in the back of the work, the resulting cable will have a right-hand twist. If the stitches are held in front, a left-twisting stitch can be made. Cable needles are available in many different materials and sizes.

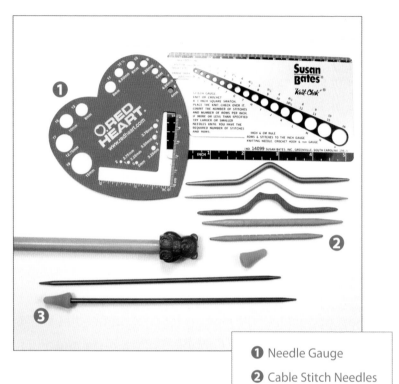

Needle Gauge: This is a valuable instrument for checking the correct size of any needle even if the size is actually stamped on the needle. These sizers are made from a flat piece of plastic or metal with holes of various sizes that correspond to needle sizes. Circular needles and double-points are usually not marked, so once they are removed from their wrappers, the only way you can determine size is to use a needle gauge. Many of these instruments also come with a knitting gauge as part of the package. For more information on gauge, see page 39.

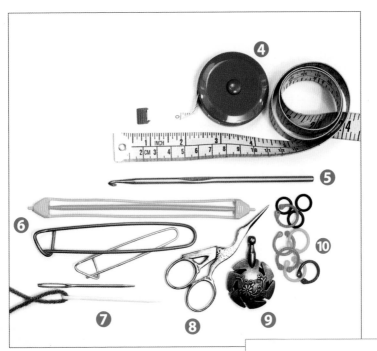

Small Scissors: Use these to cut the yarn when necessary. Never tear the yarn as this could stretch the fibers.

Yarn Cutter: With a built-in blade cutter, the yarn and thread can be easily and safely cut with any of the grooves. For knitters who travel by airplane, this is a most valuable replacement for scissors, which are sometimes confiscated.

Crochet hook: Even if you don't plan to crochet, a crochet hook can be extremely useful for picking up dropped stitches.

Stitch Holders: Use these to hold stitches that are to be bound off or worked in some other way at a future point in the pattern.

Yarn Needle: A needle with a large eye and a blunt end that is used to sew pieces together and to sew in yarn ends.

Tape Measure: Use this to check your gauge and to measure your knitting. It is a good idea to have one that reads in both centimeters and inches.

Stitch Markers: These are used to mark your place in a row or round, or to keep your place at the beginning of each round when you are working with double-points or a circular needle. They slip from needle to needle as you work. You can also use a loop of a contrasting color yarn.

Point Protectors: These are useful to keep your knitting from slipping off your needle when you lay your work down. They are also very useful if you want to use your double-points as straight needles.

Yarn

One of the most confusing things for new knitters is to choose a yarn from the vast choices that there are today. Which is the yarn that will work up quickly? Which is the yarn that will look lovely as a warm sweater? Which is the yarn to use for making a baby's blanket?

Several years ago the members of the Craft Yarn Council joined together to try to set up some guidelines for the marketplace. To help consumers select the right materials for a project, they set up the following standard yarn weight system because even different fibers have a common denominator: weight.

WEIGHTS

Yarn is classified by weight, which really refers to its thickness. Yarns can be so very thin that they are used to make lace, or as fat as your little finger.

Here are the six most popular categories and the logos used to indicate each category:

Sock, Fingering, Baby Yarn. This is the yarn most often used for baby items and socks. There are 6.75 to 8 stitches per inch on sizes 1 to 3 (2.25 mm to 3.25 mm) knitting needles.

Sport, Baby Yarn. ("Sport" has nothing to do with athletic events; it is used rather as in women's sportswear.) This yarn is thicker than baby weight yarn, and works for socks, shawls, wraps and accessories. There are 5.75 to 6.5 stitches per inch on sizes 3 to 5 (3.25 mm to 3.75 mm) knitting needles.

DK, Light Worsted Weight Yarn. This yarn is just a bit thicker than Sport Weight and is slightly lighter than the Medium Weight yarn.

There are 5½ to 6 stitches per inch on sizes 5 to 7 (3.75 mm to 4.5 mm) knitting needles. The name derives from Worstead, a village in the English county of Norfolk. This village, together with North Walsham and Aylsham, became a manufacturing center for yarn and cloth after weavers from Flanders immigrated to Norfolk in the 12th century.

Worsted, Afghan, Aran yarns. The most popular and most commonly used yarn, this is only slightly heavier than the yarn in the Number 3 category. It is used for afghans, sweaters, hats, scarves, gloves and almost anything else a knitter might want to make. There are 5 to 5½ stitches per inch on sizes 7 to 9 (4.5 mm to 5.5 mm) knitting needles.

Tip: 4-ply yarn is a term often used mistakenly to refer to worsted weight yarn. All yarn is made up of a number of plies, or strands, that are twisted together to make the strand you will work with. Baby Weight yarn can be made of four plies, and Worsted Weight yarn can be made of just two plies; it all depends upon the thickness of each ply. So just because a yarn is made of four plies does not mean it is Worsted Weight.

BULKY 5  Chunky, Craft, Rug. These yarns are about twice as thick as the Worsted Weight yarns. Use large needles, and this yarn can work up very, very quickly. It is used for throws, felted items and heavy sweaters. There are 3 to 3$\frac{1}{2}$ stitches per inch on sizes 9 to 11 (5.5 mm to 8 mm) knitting needles.

SUPER BULKY 6  Bulky, Roving. These yarns are the "absolute" for creating knits in a hurry. A project made with these yarns could be completed in a few hours or at the most a few days. There are 1$\frac{1}{2}$ to 2$\frac{3}{4}$ stitches per inch on sizes 11 and larger (8 mm and larger) knitting needles.

For the complete Craft Yarn Council chart for the Standard Yarn Weight System which lists the categories and gives recommended needles, see page 96.

The weight of the yarn you use has a great deal to do with what the finished project will look like. Here are six swatches, each made with a different weight of yarn and the suggested needle size. Each square, made with the needle recommended by the Craft Yarn Council for the particular yarn weight, has the same number of stitches and the same number of rows.

SUPER BULKY 6 Lion Brand® Yarn Quick & Cozy
Size 11 needles

BULKY 5 Caron® Dazzleaire
Size 9 needles

MEDIUM 4 Red Heart® Super Saver®
Size 7 needles

LIGHT 3 Patons® Astra
Size 5 needles

FINE 2 Lion Brand® Yarn
Vanna's Glamour®
Size 3 needles

SUPER FINE 1 Red Heart® Stardust™
Size 1 needles

FIBERS

Many different types of fiber are used in yarn for knitting. Your choice of fiber is important in selecting the best product to be used in a project. Different fibers require different care in the completed project as well as determine the drape and feel of the finished work. Certain yarns are more suitable for certain uses. If you are making something for a baby or child that will require frequent washing, choose a yarn that is strong and machine washable. To be perfectly safe, trust your pattern and follow the instructions for fiber choice until you know how various fibers will wear.

Here is a description of some of the most popular yarns for knitting.

Acrylic

Acrylics are one of the most common fibers used today. This is a synthetic fiber made from acrylonitrile, which comes from coal, air, water, petroleum and limestone. The yarn, which is very resilient and moderately strong, has a good resistance to sunlight and will last through many launderings.

Angora

The yarn comes from the Angora rabbit and is gently harvested during the rabbit's natural molting process. Eight times warmer than sheep wool, it is so light that it provides warmth without weight. The fiber lacks elasticity so it is sometimes blended with sheep wool to give the yarn a bit of stretch.

Bamboo

Bamboo is a grass that can be spun into a fiber. Since it can be harvested without killing the plant, and it only takes a few months before it is ready to be harvested again, it is an environmentally friendly choice. The yarn is cool and silky, soft to the touch and works up beautifully in anything where a drape is desired.

Cashmere

One of the most exotic and rarest fibers, cashmere is the soft undercoat of the Kashmir goat. It is a soft, lightweight and warm yarn that maintains its softness in a variety of weights. It is such a delicate yarn that it is often blended with wool to make it more durable. Because the goat only produces a few ounces of yarn each year, cashmere remains one of the most expensive of fibers.

Cotton

Cotton is a soft, staple fiber that grows around the seeds of the cotton plant. Although the yarn is non-allergenic, moisture absorbing and very strong, it is heavy and dense and contains a limited amount of elasticity. It actually is weaker than silk or linen but stronger than wool. Mercerized cotton, which is produced by adding caustic acid to the cotton, is stronger and is produced in a variety of beautiful colors.

Linen

Linen, which is made from the fibers of the flax plant, is naturally crisp, strong and lustrous. It is not soft, which discourages many knitters. However, when it is blended with other fibers such as wool, it retains its silkiness. It is durable and stronger than any other fiber and absorbs moisture.

Microfibers

This is the name for synthetic fibers that measure less than one denier. The most common types are made from polyester or nylon or a combination of the two. Because the fibers are so fine, the properties of the regular sized fibers are changed. The spun yarns have more drape and a very soft feel, but they do not lose their yarn structure. Garments made with microfibers do not sag or droop. Microfiber yarns feel more like natural fibers than regular synthetic yarns. The yarn is much more heat sensitive, however, and a project made with microfibers should never be touched with an iron nor placed in a clothes dryer.

Mohair

Mohair comes from the coat of the Angora goat, and is both durable and resilient. Known for its high luster and sheen, it is often used in fiber blends to add these qualities to other yarns. The yarn is also warm and like wool has great insulating properties. Mohair is soft and fuzzy, but it can be very irritating to the skin. Therefore, mohair sweaters are often lined with silk or cotton, or the mohair yarn is mixed with other fibers for comfort.

Nylon

Nylon is the generic name for a whole group of synthetic polymers known as polyamides. Nylon was the first synthetic fiber to be made entirely from coal, water and air. Nylon is lightweight but strong and very washable. It is elastic, does not stretch or shrink unless it is subjected to very high temperatures. Nylon is often combined with wool to give wool strength and elasticity especially in sock yarns.

Polyester

Polyester is another synthetic fiber which is strong and resistant to stretching and shrinking while remaining very washable. It is often combined with other fibers to add strength and resilience. Combined with cotton, it makes the cotton more absorbent while a combination of polyester and wool helps the wool maintain its shape in all types of weather. When it is added to rayon and nylon, the resulting yarns have better drape and are strong, durable and easy to launder.

Rayon

Rayon is not a natural fiber, but it is made from naturally occurring ingredients that have required extensive processing before the threads are created. It is actually the oldest manufactured fiber, having been in production since the 1880s. Rayon is highly absorbent, can be hand washed and dries quickly. It drapes well and is so easy to dye that rayon is available in a variety of colors. The thread is frequently blended with other fibers and often is used instead of silk. The yarn is slippery, however, and requires a bit of skill in working with it.

Silk

Although silk is not strictly an animal fiber, it does have some of the same properties because it has a protein structure. It doesn't conduct heat so silk is an excellent insulator and will serve to keep the recipient of a silk garment cool in the summer and warm in the winter. Silk yarn will create a light, velvety-soft ultra smooth garment that will not shrink or stretch.

Soy

Creating yarn from vegetable fibers, like soy, is not new; actually cotton and linen are made from vegetable fibers. Recently with the new interest from environmentalists in the development of eco-friendly products, new soy yarns have arrived on the market. Although there are yarns made of 100% soy, most soy yarns are blended with wool or acrylic. These yarns have a beautiful sheen and drape beautifully.

Wool

While the term wool is used often to mean any fiber shorn from an animal, to knitters the term "wool" refers to the fiber that comes from sheep. This is probably the most durable and versatile of all fibers used in knitting. A wool garment retains its shape and resists wrinkles so it is able to absorb perspiration, releasing it gradually thereby making a wool garment comfortable year around. Wool is easily dyed and flame retardant. Wool should be washed and dried by hand; however, if washed in very hot water and dried in a dryer, the wool will felt. This may be desirable since "felting" is a technique that produces interesting results. Superwashed wool has been treated to prevent felting and can be washed in a washer.

Merino Wool was originally a term used to describe wool from merino sheep in Spain. This was the finest and softest wool. Today merino wool comes from other places, and the term is used to describe the very best soft wool.

CHOOSING YOUR YARN: THE BALL BAND

When you go to buy yarn, you will find yourself surrounded by all kinds of yarns in different fibers, in various weights besides being in the color you want. If you can find a knowledgeable sales assistant to help you, you're in luck. If, however, you are alone, don't despair. Almost every yarn in the store can help you because most yarns are enclosed with a ball band that tells you everything you need to know about that particular yarn. Once you have learned to read a ball band, you'll never be afraid to buy yarn again.

Yarn is packaged differently by different manufacturers and by the type of yarn. Sometimes it is sold as a hank, which is a coil of loosely wound yarn. That type of yarn will require your winding it into a ball before you begin to knit. Some yarn is pre-wound into a ball or skein, and the ball band will often give you information on how to pull the yarn onto your needle. Almost all yarn, however it is packaged, will have a ball band with the important information.

While a salesperson in a store can help you with this information, if you learn to read a ball band, you will always be able to learn everything about a yarn.

The ball band label will tell you all you need to know to make an intelligent choice of yarn. It will give you the name of the manufacturer and the manufacturer's web address, the name of the yarn and its fiber content, the amount of yarn in the ball and where the yarn was made.

The label will give you the yarn weight category symbol that was discussed on pages 22-24 along with a chart showing what size of needle will work best to obtain the necessary gauge, which shows how many stitches and rows it will take to make a 4" swatch. (See pages 39-42 for a further explanation of gauge.) It will also tell you how to take care of a project made with the yarn.

(continued on page 34)

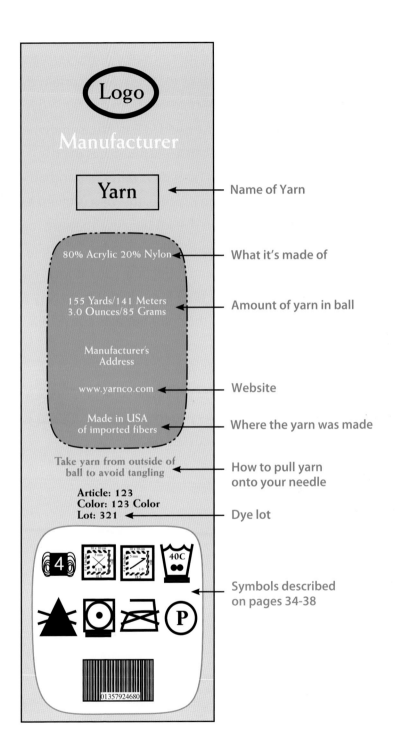

Logo

Manufacturer

Yarn ← Name of Yarn

80% Acrylic 20% Nylon ← What it's made of

155 Yards/141 Meters
3.0 Ounces/85 Grams ← Amount of yarn in ball

Manufacturer's
Address

www.yarnco.com ← Website

Made in USA
of imported fibers ← Where the yarn was made

Take yarn from outside of
ball to avoid tangling ← How to pull yarn
onto your needle

Article: 123
Color: 123 Color
Lot: 321 ← Dye lot

← Symbols described
on pages 34-38

01357924680

The label will also give you the specific color of the yarn along with the dye lot. It is very important that you make certain that all of the yarn for a specific project comes from the same dye lot. Yarns that have dye lots listed are dyed in batches, somewhere about 3,000 skeins at a time. Because each batch is dyed individually, and factors such as humidity, water pH, and others can have an effect on the dyeing process, the yarn is given a dye lot number. Some yarns have no dye lot because they are made from colored fiber purchased from a fiber supplier. The color is injected as the fiber is formed, and it becomes an intrinsic part of the fiber itself. So long as the fiber is made the same way and provided by the same supplier, the color remains consistent.

The final part of the label gives you symbols which tell you about the yarn you are using. The first symbol shows you the size or weight of the yarn as discussed on pages 22-24.

The next symbol suggests the size of needle you should use and the gauge that you should attain using this needle. (See pages 39-42 for an explanation of gauge.)

The "8 US" and the "5 mm" indicate that the average knitter should use size 8 (5 mm) knitting needles to work with this yarn. The label now tells you that with your size 8 needle, you should make a 4" x 4" (10 x 10 cm) square in which you will probably achieve 24 rows and each row will be 16 stitches. That says that with this yarn, you will get about 4 stitches to an inch (16÷4=4). Knitters should always make their own gauge swatch using the suggested gauge as a jumping-off point!

The same information is given in the second square for crochet.

In the last part of the label, there is a list of laundering and dry cleaning symbols. Here are some of the most popular symbols:

SYMBOL	MEANING
	Machine Wash, Normal: Garment made from this yarn may be laundered through use of a machine designed for this purpose.
	**Machine Wash, Cold:** Initial water temperature should not exceed 30° centigrade or 86° Fahrenheit.
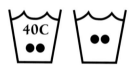	**Machine Wash, Warm:** Initial water temperature should not exceed 40° centigrade or 104° Fahrenheit.
	Machine Wash, Gentle or Delicate: Garment made from this yarn may be machine laundered only on the setting designed for gentle agitation and/or reduced time for delicate items.
	**Hand Wash:** Garment made from this yarn may be laundered through use of water, detergent or soap and gentle hand manipulation. Required water temperature is indicated by the number of dots.

SYMBOL	MEANING

 Do Not Wash: Garment made from this yarn may not be safely laundered by any process.

 Do Not Bleach: No bleach product may be used. A garment made from this yarn is not colorfast or structurally able to withstand any bleach.

 Tumble Dry, Normal: Garment made from this yarn may be dried in a machine used at the hottest available temperature setting.

 Tumble Dry, Normal, Low Heat: Garment made from this yarn may be dried in a machine regularly used at a maximum of Low Heat setting.

 Do Not Tumble Dry: Garment made from this yarn should not be dried in a machine dryer.

 Dry Flat: Garment made from this yarn should be laid out horizontally for drying.

SYMBOL	MEANING

 Iron, Low: Garment made from this yarn can be ironed, either steam or dry, but may be done at Low setting (110° centigrade, 230° Fahrenheit).

 Do Not Iron: Garment made from this yarn may not be smoothed or finished with an iron.

 Dry Clean, Any Solvent: Garment made from this yarn may be dry cleaned in any solvent.

 Dry Clean Petroleum Solvent Only: Garment made from this yarn may be dry cleaned in a petroleum solvent only.

 Do Not Dry Clean: Garment made from this yarn may not be commercially dry cleaned.

Note: Even if the label says that the yarn is washable, either by machine or by hand, it's a good idea to test the yarn before you complete an entire project that may require frequent washing. You might want to try using the gauge swatch that you make according to the instructions on page 41.

The Importance of Gauge

Many new knitters tend to shy away from gauge as if it were a dirty word. Gauge, however, is the most important word in the knitter's dictionary. It is the most important lesson a knitter can learn!

As a knitter, if you want the garments that you will make to fit properly; if you want the afghans to be the correct size; and if you want to be sure that you have enough yarn to complete a project, then you need to follow the gauge given in a pattern.

Gauge simply means the number of stitches per inch, and the number of rows per inch that result from a specified yarn worked with needles in a specified size. However, since everyone knits differently—some loosely, some tightly, some in between—the measurements of individual work can vary greatly, even when the knitters use the same pattern, the same size needles and the same size yarn.

The needle sizes given in instructions are only guides. You should never go ahead with a project without making a 4" square to check your gauge. The knitter has the responsibility to make sure to achieve the gauge specified in the pattern. You may need to use a different size needle from that specified in the pattern. Those needle sizes given in instructions are just guides, and they should never be used without first making a gauge swatch.

Here's how you make a swatch to check your gauge. At the beginning of every knit pattern, you'll find a gauge given such as the one below. The pattern has called for size 8 (5mm) knitting needles.

Gauge
16 stitches = 4" in stockinette stitch
(knit one row, purl one row)
24 rows = 4"

This actually means that you will work your gauge swatch in stockinette stitch and will try to achieve a gauge of 4 stitches and 6 rows to an inch. You must make a gauge swatch of at least 4" square to adequately test your work. Cast on 16 stitches and work in stockinette stitch (knit one row; purl one row) for 24 rows. For more information on stockinette stitch, see page 86. Loosely bind off all stitches.

Place the swatch on a flat surface and pin it out. Be careful not to stretch the knitting. Measure the outside edges; the sample should be a 4" square.

Now measure the center 2" and count the actual stitches and rows per inch.

If you have more stitches or rows per inch than listed in the pattern, make another gauge swatch with larger size needles.

If you have fewer stitches or rows per inch than specified, make another swatch with smaller size needles.

Sometimes you may find that you have the correct stitch gauge, but you are unable to get the row gauge even with another set of needles. If so, don't be concerned; the stitch gauge is more important than the row gauge, and if you get the stitch gauge to work, your knitting will work. The only place where an incorrect row gauge might be a problem is in knitting raglan sweaters where both gauges must be perfect.

Once you have begun a pattern, it's not a bad idea to check your gauge every few inches. Sometimes if you become very relaxed, your knitting can become looser; if you become tense, your knitting can become tighter. To keep your gauge, you might need to change needles in the middle of a project.

Making gauge swatches before starting a project takes time, and it is a bother. But if you miss this important step, you'll never be able to create beautiful projects that fit.

Reading a Pattern

Knitting patterns are actually written in a special language which consists of abbreviations, symbols, asterisks, parentheses, colons, daggers and brackets. This special "shorthand" is used so that instructions don't take up too much space. In the beginning they may seem confusing, but once you learn them, you will have no trouble in following them.

SKILL LEVELS

Before beginning a project, it is a good idea to find out the skill level of a pattern. Here are the standard skill level icons developed by the Craft Yarn Council. Each of these icons, which appear with knitting patterns in books, magazines, leaflets, on yarn labels or on web sites, is a horizontal bar divided into four sections. When one section of the bar is shaded, it indicates a beginner pattern; four shaded sections indicate a pattern for experienced knitters.

BEGINNER

Beginner: Projects for first-time knitters using basic knit and purl stitches. Minimal shaping.

EASY

Easy: Projects using basic stitches, repetitive stitch patterns, simple color changes, and simple shaping and finishing.

INTERMEDIATE

Intermediate: Projects with a variety of stitches, such as basic cables and lace, simple intarsia, double-point needles and knitting in the round techniques, mid-level shaping and finishing.

EXPERIENCED

Experienced: Projects using advanced techniques and stitches, such as short rows, Fair Isle, more intricate intarsia, cables, lace patterns, and numerous color changes.

STANDARD ABBREVIATIONS

alt	alternate
approx	approximately
beg	beginning
bet	between
bl	back loop
BO	bind off
CC	contrasting color
cm	centimeter
cn	cable needle
CO	cast on
cont	continue
dec	decrease
dpn	double-point needles
fig	figure
fl	front loop
foll	follow(ing)
g	gram(s)
inc	increase(ing)
K	knit
K2tog	knit two stitches together
Kwise	knitwise
LH	left hand
Lp(s)	loop(s)
m	meter(s)

STANDARD ABBREVIATIONS

M1	increase one stitch
MC	main color
mm	millimeter(s)
oz	ounces
P	purl
P2tog	purl two stitches together
patt	pattern
PM	place marker
prev	previous
PSSO	pass the slipped stitch over
Pwise	purlwise
rem	remain(ing)
rep	repeat(ing)
RH	right hand
rnd(s)	round(s)
RS	right side
sk	skip
skp	slip, knit, pass stitch over

STANDARD ABBREVIATIONS

sl	slip
sl1K	sl 1 knitwise
sl1P	sl 1 purlwise
sl st (s)	slip stitch(es)
sp(s)	space(s)
SSK	slip, slip, knit
st(s)	stitch(es)
stock st	stockinette stitch
St st	stockinette stitch
tbl	through back loop
tog	together
WS	wrong side
wyib	with yarn in back of needle
wyif	with yarn in front of needle
yd(s)	yard(s)
yf	yarn in front of needle
yrn	yarn around needle
YO	yarn over the needle

STANDARD SYMBOLS

* An asterisk (or double asterisks**) in a pattern row, indicates a portion of instructions to be used more than once. For instance, "rep from * three times" means that after working the instructions once, you must work them again three times for a total of 4 times in all.

† A dagger (or double daggers ††) indicates that those instructions will be repeated again later in the same row or round.

: The number after a colon tells you the number of stitches you will have when you have completed the row or round.

( ) Parentheses enclose instructions which are to be worked the number of times following the parentheses. For instance, "(K1, P2) 3 times" means that you knit one stitch and then purl two stitches, three times.
Parentheses often set off or clarify a group of stitches to be worked into the same space or stitch.

[ ] Brackets and ( ) parentheses are also used to give you additional information. For instance, "(rem sts are left unworked)."

STANDARD TERMS

Finish off: This means to end your piece by cutting your yarn several inches beyond last st worked and pulling the yarn end through the last loop remaining on the needle. This will prevent the work from unraveling.

Continue in Pattern (Patt) as Established: This means to follow the pattern stitch as it has been set up, working any increases or decreases in such a way that the pattern remains the same as it was established.

Work even: This means that the work is continued in the pattern as established without increasing or decreasing.

Right Side: This means the side of the garment that will be seen.

Wrong Side: This means the side of the garment that is inside when the garment is worn.

Right Front: This means the part of the garment that will be worn on the right side of the body.

Left Front: This means the part of the garment that will be worn on the left side of the body.

The patterns in most books and magazines published in the United States use the knitting terminology that is used in the United States. Terms which may have different equivalents in other parts of the world are listed below.

United States	International
gauge	tension
skip	miss
yarn over (YO)	yarn forward (yfwd)
bind off	cast off

Working a Pattern

If you'd like to try your hand at reading and working a pattern, here are patterns as they would appear in a book, a magazine, or online (except we've addded breaks and spacing for clarity). To help you, we've given you a "translation" of several lines to explain what is happening. It's almost as if you had a knitting friend sitting with you as you work.

If you've never worked a published pattern before, you might want to start with the easier ones—the Delightful Dish Cloth or the Wonderful Washcloth—before attempting the Hat on page 59.

DELIGHTFUL DISHCLOTH

Pattern

⬤☐☐☐ **BEGINNER**

Size

About 9¹/₂" x 9¹/₂"
(24.1 cm x 24.1 cm)

Materials

MEDIUM 4

Worsted Weight
cotton yarn [100% cotton,
2.5 ounces, 120 yards
(70.9 grams, 109 meters)
per ball]
1 ball blue
Size 7 (4.5 mm) knitting
needles (or size required
for gauge)

Note: *Photographed model
made with Lily® Sugar 'n Cream®
#00026 Light Blue*

Translation

See the definition of "Beginner" on
page 44.

Here is the information about the yarn
that was used to make the photographed
model. The chart on page 96 will explain
more about number 4 yarn. This tells you
how many ounces or yards come on each
ball or skein of the chosen yarn brand so
that you can determine how much yarn
you would need if you chose another
number 4 yarn. Make certain that whatever
yarn you use is 100% cotton.

Gauge

18 sts = 4" (10 cm) in garter st (knit each row)

See pages 40-42 for information on determining the correct gauge. You may be required to use smaller or larger knitting needles to attain the proper gauge.

If you need help in working garter stitch, see pages 82-84.

Instructions

CO 4 sts.

Cast on 4 sts. To do this, make a slip knot and then cast on an additional 3 stitches loosely so that the stitches are loose enough to be worked into. For help in casting on, see pages 78-81.

Part One

Row 1: Knit.

In Part One, you are increasing each row until there are 54 stitches on the needle. For help in increasing in knitting, see pages 90-91.

Row 2: Knit into front and back of each stitch: 8 sts.
Row 3: Knit.

Row 2 tells you to increase by knitting into the front and back of each stitch. This will give you 8 stitches on your needle. For help in working into the front and back of a stitch, see page 90. At the end of the row, you will see a colon and a number after the colon. The number will tell you how many stitches you now have on your needle.

Row 4: K4, YO, knit to end of row.

In Row 4, you are increasing by making an eyelet in the knitting by working a YO (a yarn over). Start the row by knitting 4 stitches, then work a yarn over, and continue knitting to the end of the row. You will have increased the row by one stitch. If you need help in working a YO (yarn over) see pages 90-91.

Rows 5-49: Rep Row 4 until there are 54 sts on the needle. Do not BO.

You will work a total of 49 rows. When you have 54 stitches, do not bind off. Do not end the knitting. Continue to Part Two.

Part Two

Row 1: K4, YO, K2tog; knit to end of row.

In Part Two, you will decrease in each row until there are 9 stitches left on the needle. Rows 1 and 2 do not have decreases.

Row 2: Rep Row 1.

You merely knit 4 stitches, work a yarn over and then knit two stitches together (K2tog). For instructions on making a K2tog, see page 88.

Row 3: K3, K2tog, YO, K2tog; knit to end of row.
Repeat Row 3 until there are 9 sts on the needle.

In Row 3, you begin decreasing. Knit 3, then knit two stitches together (K2tog), work a yarn over (YO) and another K2tog (knit two stitches together) and continue knitting to the end of the row.

When you have 9 stitches on the needle, do not bind off. Continue to Part 3.

Part Three

Row 1: K3, K2tog, K4: 8 sts.
Row 2: Knit across.
Row 3: *K2tog; rep from * across: 4 sts.

In Part Three, you decrease again, ending the work with 4 stitches, the same number of stitches that you cast on at the start.

BO.

Bind off the remaining four stitches. For help in binding off, see pages 91-92.

WONDERFUL WASHCLOTH

Pattern

◼☐☐☐ **BEGINNER**

Translation

See the definition of "Beginner" on page 44

Size

About 10¹/₂" x 10¹/₂"
(26.67 cm x 26.67 cm)

Materials

Worsted Weight **MEDIUM 4**
   cotton yarn [100% cotton,
   2.5 ounces, 120 yards (70.9
   grams, 109 meters) per ball]
   1 ball yellow
Size 7 (4.5 mm) knitting
   needles (or size required
   for gauge)

Note: *Photographed model
made with Lily® Sugar 'n Cream®
#00010 Yellow*

Here is the information about the yarn that was used to make the photographed model. The chart on page 96 will explain more about number 4 yarn. This tells you how many ounces or yards come on each ball or skein of the chosen yarn brand so that you can determine how much yarn you would need if you chose another number 4 yarn. Make certain that whatever yarn you use is 100% cotton.

Gauge

5 sts = 2" in patt

Pattern

Row 1: P5, K3.

Row 2: K5, P3.

Instructions

CO 39 stitches

Row 1: Knit across.

Row 2: Knit across.

Row 3: Knit across.

Row 4 (wrong side): K2; purl across to last 2 sts, K2.

Row 5: K5; *P5, K3; rep from * across to last 2 sts, K2.

See pages 40-42 for information on determining the correct gauge. You may be required to use smaller or larger knitting needles to attain the proper gauge. The gauge here is given over a pattern of two rows. Work your swatch over 8 stitches. For help in working the knit stitch and the purl stitch, see pages 82-86.

Cast on 39 stitches. To do this, make a slip knot and then cast on an additional 38 stitches loosely so that the stitches are loose enough to be worked into.

For help in casting on, see pages 78-81.

The pattern begins with three rows of knitting to make a border along the bottom.

Each row now begins and ends with 2 knit stitches. These are selvage stitches and will make a nice border along the sides.

Begin Row 5 by knitting 5 stitches. Then there is an asterisk (*) followed by instructions to purl 5 stitches and to knit 3 stitches. The instructions now tell you to repeat the instructions after the asterisk (P5, K3) to the last 2 stitches, which are now knitted for the border.

Row 6: K2, P3; *K5, P3; rep from * across to last 2 sts, K2.

You work Row 6 by starting with knitting 2 stitches, and purling 3 stitches. Then you repeat everything after the asterisk (*) across the row to the last 2 stitches, which are knitted for the border.

Row 7: K5; *P5, K3; rep from * across to last 2 sts, K2.
Row 8: Rep Row 4.
Row 9: K2, P4; *K3, P5; rep from * across, ending last rep with P4, K2.
Row 10: K6; *P3, K5; rep from * across, ending last rep with K6.
Row 11: K2, P4; *K3, P5; rep from * across, ending last rep with P4, K2.
Repeat Rows 4 through 11 eight times.

In the next rows work the instructions, always repeating the instructions after the asterisk (*) across the row.

Knit 3 rows.

End by working 3 rows of knitting to make a border along the top.

BO.

Bind off the stitches. For help in binding off, see pages 91-92.

HAT

Pattern

◼◼◻◻ **EASY**

Finished Size

Fits 21" (53.5 cm) head
   circumference

Materials

Worsted Weight yarn **MEDIUM 4**
   [96% acrylic, 4% other fibers,
   3 ounces 160 yards (85 grams,
   46 meters) per skein]
   1 skein white
Size 8 (5 mm) knitting needles
   (or size required for gauge)
Yarn needle

Note: *Photographed model made
with Red Heart® Super Saver®
#311 White*

Translation

See the definition of "Easy" on page 44.

Here is information about the yarn that
was used to make the photographed
model. The chart on page 96 will explain
more about number 4 yarn. This tells you
how many ounces or yards come on each
skein of the chosen yarn brand so that you
can determine how much yarn you would
need if you chose another number 4 yarn.

Gauge

19 sts = 4" in pattern

Often instructions for a special pattern are given; if no instructions are given, the pattern is the first few rows; here rows 1 and 2.

Instructions

Starting at bottom of hat, CO 87 sts loosely.

Cast on 87 stitches. To do this, make a slip knot and then cast on an additional 86 stitches loosely so that the stitches are loose enough to be worked into.

If you need help casting on, see pages 78-81.

Row 1(right side): K1; *P2, K2; rep from * across.

This tells you that this row is the right side and means: knit one stitch. The asterisk (*) tells you to repeat purl 2 and knit 2 across the row. If you need help in working a knit stitch and a purl stitch, see pages 82-86.

Row 2: *K2, P2; rep from * across to the last 3 sts, K2, P1.

In Row 2, work the stitches after the asterisk (*) across the row until you come to the last 3 stitches. Work the 3 stitches by knitting 2 stitches and purling 1 stitch.

Rep Rows 1 and 2 until piece measures 10³/₄" from CO row, ending by working a wrong-side row.

Repeat these 2 rows until your piece measures 10³/₄" from the cast on row. You should end by working a wrong side row.

Shape Top

Now you will begin shaping your project. As you work each row, you will begin decreasing stitches until you have only 13 stitches left on your needle. At the end of a row with a decrease, you will see a colon and a number after the colon. The number will tell you how many stitches you now have on your needle.

Row 1: K1; *P2, K2tog, P2, K2; rep from * across, ending last rep with P2, K2tog, P2: 76 sts.

In Row 1, you begin your decreasing. Each group of stitches after the asterisk will be reduced from 8 stitches to 7 stitches. The decrease is made by knitting 2 stitches together, called a K2tog. For help in making a K2tog, see page 88.

At the end of the row, you will see the colon with the number 76 after it. This indicates that you will now have 76 stitches on your needles.

Row 2: K2, P1; *K2, P2, K2, P1; rep from * across to last 3 sts; K2, P1.

Row 2 and all of the even rows—except for the final row (Row 12)—have no decreases.

Work across the 76 stitches you now have on your needles.

Row 3: K1; *P2, K1, P2, K2tog; rep from * across to last 5 sts, P2, K1, P2: 66 sts.

In Row 3, the groups of 7 stitches after the asterisk are reduced to 6 stitches. The total number of stitches on the needles, listed after the colon, is 66.

Row 4: K2; *P1, K2; rep from * across to last st, K1.

Row 4 has no decreases. Work across the 66 stitches on the needles.

Row 5: K1; *P2tog, K1, P2, K1; rep from * across to last 5 sts, P2tog, K1, P2: 55 sts.

In Row 5, each group of stitches after the asterisk will be reduced from 6 stitches to 5 stitches. The decrease here is made by a purl 2 together (P2tog), which is worked the same as a K2tog (page 88) except that the needle is inserted from right to left into the fronts of the next 2 stitches, and then they are purled together as if they were 1 stitch.

At the end of the row, you will see the colon with the number 55 after it. This indicates that you now have 55 stitches on the needles.

Row 6: K2, *P1, K1, P1, K2; rep from * to last 3 sts, P1, K1, P1.

Row 6 has no decreases. Work across the 55 stitches on the needle.

Row 7: *K1, P1, K1, P2tog; rep from * to last 5 sts, (K1, P1) twice, K1: 45 sts.

Row 8: K1; *K1, P1; rep from * to end of row.

Some of these rows have parentheses enclosing instructions which are to be worked the number of times following the parentheses. For instance in Row 7 (K1, P1) twice means that you knit 1 stitch, then purl 1 stitch, twice, working 4 stitches.

Row 9: (K1, P1) twice; *sl 1, K2tog, PSSO, (P1, K1) twice, P1; rep from * to last st, K1: 35 sts.

Row 10: K1; *K1, P1; rep from * to end of row.

Row 11: (K1, P1) twice; *sl 1, K2tog, PSSO, P1, K1, P1; rep from * to last st, K1: 25 sts.

Row 12: K1; *P1, sl 1, K2tog, PSSO; rep from * to end of row: 13 sts.

In Row 9, you will work another method of decreasing which is explained on page 89. In this method you will slip 1 stitch, knit 2 stitches together and pass the slip stitches over the knit stitch (sl 1, K2tog, PSSO).

Cut yarn, leaving a long end. Thread yarn into a yarn needle and draw end through rem sts and fasten securely. Sew center back seam.

In this method you do not bind off your stitches, but you thread the long end of the yarn into a large needle and draw the yarn through the remaining stitches and pull the yarn tightly. Now use the thread to sew the center back seam as shown on pages 93-94. Some knitters like to reverse the seam for the amount of the knitting that will be the cuff turnback.

Correcting Mistakes

Even expert knitters occasionally make mistakes, but they know how to correct them.

Before you correct any stitches, be certain that all of your stitches are sitting correctly on the needle.

Every stitch has a front and a back arm. All stitches should be sitting on the needle with the right arm in front of the needle. If a stitch is made with the left arm in front of the needle, your stitch will be twisted.

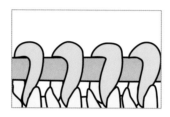

DROPPED STITCHES

The mistake that many knitters make is a dropped stitch. That's when a stitch slips off the needle before you've knitted or purled it. A dropped stitch must be picked up; otherwise the stitch will run down the length of the entire piece.

If you catch the dropped stitch before it has run down more than one row, you can probably ease it back on the needle. However, if it has run down several rows, you can use a crochet hook to work the stitch back up to its place on the needle.

ON THE KNIT SIDE

Insert a crochet hook into the dropped stitch from front to back, under the horizontal strand in the row above.

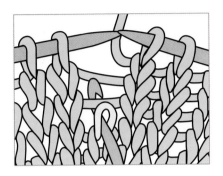

Hook the horizontal strand above and pull it through the loop on the crochet hook.

Continue doing this until you reach the working row on the needle, then move the loop from the crochet hook to the left needle. Be very careful not to twist it. Make certain that the "arm" is sitting correctly on the needle.

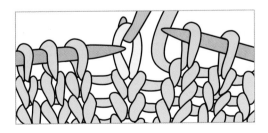

ON THE PURL SIDE

Move the horizontal strand in front of the dropped stitch. Insert the crochet hook into the dropped stitch from back to front over the horizontal strand. Hook the horizontal strand and pull through the loop on the crochet hook.

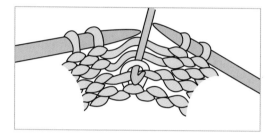

UNDOING ROWS OF STITCHES

If you find a mistake down a row or two, you can still correct your mistake. Unravel the stitches one-by-one by putting the left needle into the row below and undoing the stitch above until the mistake is corrected.

If the mistake is several rows below, very carefully slip all of the stitches off the needle and unravel every row down to the row in which the mistake has happened. Then unravel this row, stitch by stitch, placing each stitch back on the needle in the proper position. Be sure that you do not twist the stitch and that all stitches are sitting correctly with knit stitches on knit rows and purl stitches on purl rows.

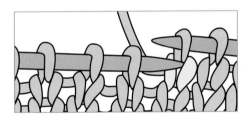

JOINING YARN

Never add yarn in the middle of a row (unless the pattern requires this for a color change). New yarn should only be added at the beginning of a row. If you have run out of yarn and wish to add new yarn, tie a new strand around the old strand, making a knot at the edge of the work and leaving at least 6" on both strands. Continue to knit with the new strand. When you have finished the project, weave in all of the ends.

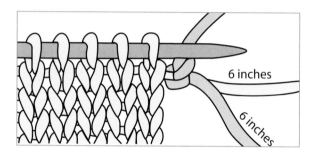

6 inches

6 inches

Making Fringe and Tassels

A wonderful way to finish a project is to add fringe or tassels. Here are instructions for both.

FRINGE

Basic Instructions

Cut a piece of cardboard about 6" wide and half as long or as specified in the instructions for strands, plus $1/2$" for trimming allowance. Wind the yarn loosely and evenly lengthwise around the cardboard. When the card is filled, cut the yarn across one end. Do this several times; then begin fringing. You can wind additional strands as you need them.

Single Knot Fringe

Hold the specified number of strands for one knot of fringe together, then fold in half.

Hold the project with the right side facing you. Using a crochet hook, draw the folded ends through the space or stitch from right to wrong side.

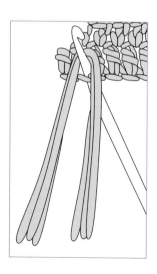

Pull the loose ends through the folded section.

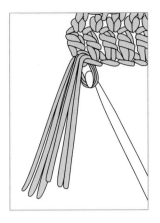

Draw the knot up firmly.

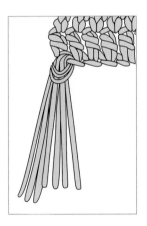

Space the knots evenly and trim the ends of the fringe.

Double Knot Fringe

Work a row of single knot fringe. Then use half the strands from one knot and half the strands from the next knot to tie a row of knots about $1^{1}/_{2}$" below the first row.

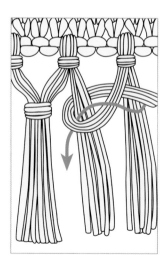

Triple Knot Fringe

Work a row of double knot fringe. Then add another row of knots.

TASSELS

Decide how long the desired tassel is going to be, and cut a piece of cardboard to use as a guide that is $1/2$" longer than desired length.

For tie, place a 12" piece of yarn across top of the guide. Wind the yarn around the guide and over the tie. Keep winding until the tassel is the desired thickness.

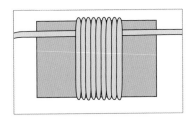

Draw the tie up tightly and knot it. Slide the yarn off the guide and cut the yarn at the bottom of the guide.

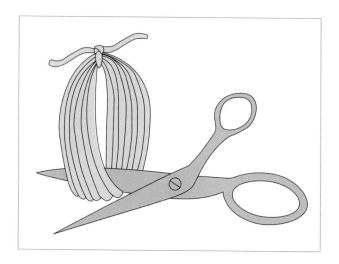

Cut another 12" yarn strip and wrap it tightly about an inch below the top of the tassel. Wrap several times and tie a secure knot. Trim the ends of the strip and the bottom of the tassel.

Refresher Course in Knitting

CASTING ON

There are many methods of casting on. Some give a nice stretchy edge; others give a firm base. If you have already been taught a method of casting on, feel free to use it. If, however, you are a beginner, try this easy method.

Step One: Make a slip knot on one needle like this: Make a loop of yarn, leaving about 6" free at one end.

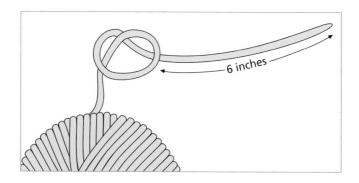

Now put the pointed end of one knitting needle through the loop and pull the yarn up from the free end to form a loop on the needle.

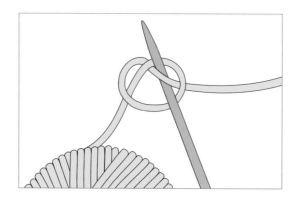

Draw the yarn firmly, but not too tightly, to form a slip knot on the straight part of the needle, not on the pointed end.

Now draw on the free yarn end to firm up the loop. This slip knot is the first stitch you have made.

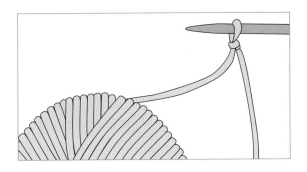

Step Two: Hold the needle with the slip knot in your right hand. With your left hand form a loop in the yarn coming from the ball like this.

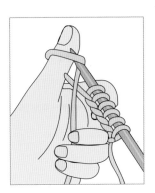

Insert the needle in your right hand into the center of the loop, then pull the yarn from the ball gently until the loop forms a snug new stitch on the right needle. You have now added another stitch, and there are two stitches on the right needle. Now make another loop in the same way, insert the right needle into it, and pull the yarn to make it snug. Keep doing this until you have sufficient stitches on the needle. Put the needle with all your stitches into your left hand.

Step Three: Now pick up the other knitting needle with your right hand, with your thumb and index finger near the point. Hold the needle firmly, but not tightly.

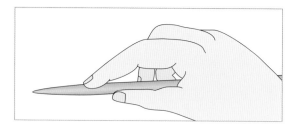

Step Four: Your right hand is in charge of controlling the yarn coming from the ball or skein. Hold it loosely across the palm of your hand with three fingers, then bring it up and over your index finger. The diagrams show how this looks from above and below your hand.

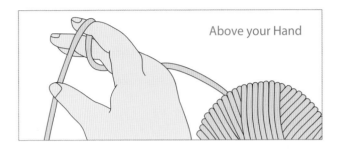

Above your Hand

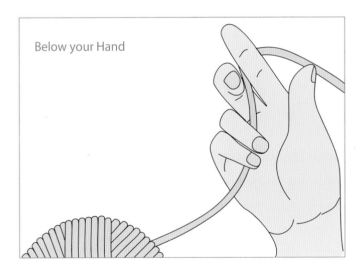

Below your Hand

THE KNIT STITCH

Now you start to work with both needles at the same time. It may feel awkward at first, but soon you will be able to do this easily.

Step One: Holding the needle with the cast-on stitches in your left hand, insert the point of the right needle from front to back into the first stitch on the left needle. Be sure to keep the right needle under the left needle.

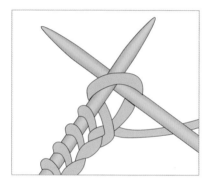

Step Two: Use your right index finger to pick up the yarn from the ball and bring it under and over the point of the right needle.

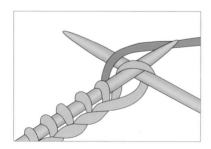

Step Three: Now draw the yarn through the slip stitch with the point of the right needle.

Step Four: Slip the loop off the left needle so that the new stitch will be entirely on the right needle.

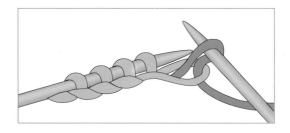

Draw the yarn from the ball gently to make the new loop snug on the needle. You should be able to slide it back and forth on the needle easily. Repeat these four steps in each stitch remaining on the left needle. When all of the stitches are on the right needle, and the left needle is free, a row has been completed. Now take the needle with the stitches and put it in your left hand with the point of the needle facing toward your right. Now you have one free needle, which you hold in your right hand.

Work another row of stitches in the same manner as the last row.

When you knit every row, it is called garter stitch, and the piece will look like this.

THE PURL STITCH

The other stitch you need to learn is called the purl stitch. Instead of inserting the point of the right needle from the front to the back under the left needle, as you do for making the knit stitch, you insert it from right to left in front of the left needle.

Step One: Insert the right needle from right to left into the first stitch on the left needle and in front of the left needle.

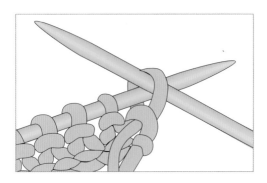

Step Two: Hold the yarn in front of the work (the side facing you), and draw it around the right needle counter clockwise.

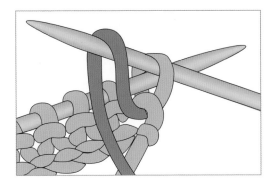

Step Three: Pull the yarn back through the stitch with the right needle.

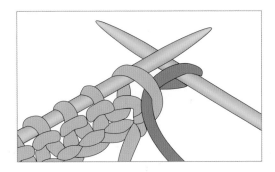

Now slide the stitch off the left needle and let it remain on the right needle. You have now made one purl stitch.

Continue to repeat these steps in each of the remaining stitches on the row.

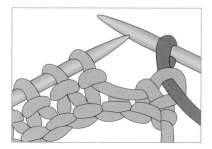

Alternating one row of knit stitches with one row of purl stitches is called Stockinette stitch, and is one of the most often used stitch patterns in knitting.

The results will look like this.

This is the knit side.   This is the purl side.

RIBBING

When alternating knit and purl stitches are combined in the same row, the result is called ribbing. This makes an elastic effect, making the knitting fit more closely such as at the neck, the bottom of a sweater, or the wrists of a mitten or glove.

Knit two stitches, then bring the yarn to the front under the tip of the needle, and purl two stitches; repeat the process across the row.

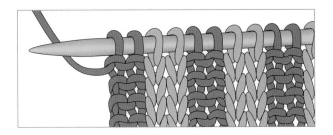

DECREASING

When your pattern asks you to decrease your stitches, you can use two techniques, either knitting two stitches together, or slipping a stitch and then passing it over a knit stitch.

Knit 2 together (k2tog)

Insert the needle through the fronts of 2 stitches on the left needle, and bring the yarn under and over the point of the needle.

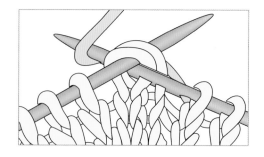

Draw the yarn through both stitches. Slip both stitches off the left needle, and one new stitch will be on the right needle. One stitch has been decreased.

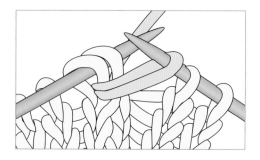

Pass slip stitch over (PSSO)

When the instructions say to slip a stitch, you merely slip the stitch from one needle to the other without working it. Insert the right needle into the stitch as if you were going to purl, even if it is a knit stitch, but instead of actually purling, slip the stitch from the left needle to the right needle.

Step 1: Slip the next stitch as if to purl.

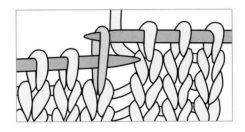

Step 2: Knit the next stitch (or stitches).

Step 3: Pass the slipped stitch over the knit stitch or stitches by using the point of the left needle inserted from back to front of stitch, to lift the slipped stitch over the next stitch or stitches and drop it off the needle.

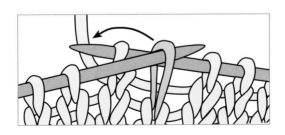

INCREASING

When your pattern asks you to increase stitches, you can do this by knitting into the front and back of the same stitch.

Step 1: Insert the tip of the right needle from front to back of a stitch. Knit it in the usual way, but do not remove the stitch from the left needle.

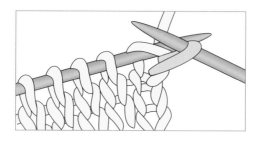

Step 2: Now insert the right needle from front to back into the back loop of the same stitch and knit it again. This time slip it off the left needle. One stitch has been increased.

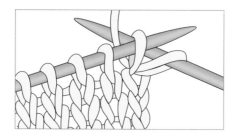

You can also add a stitch by making a YO (yarn over). This is just made by wrapping the yarn around the right needle between two stitches. The yarn over will make a hole in the knitting which might be desired especially when knitting lace.

BINDING OFF

When you are finished with a knitted piece, you need to know how to take the stitches off the needle. Because stitches in knitting are locked together, they would run all the way down to the beginning of the cast-on stitches. So binding off is used to secure them.

Begin with the right side (or knit side of stockinette pattern) facing you.

Step 1: Knit the first two stitches. Next, insert the left needle into the first of the 2 stitches, and draw it over the second stitch and drop it completely off the needle. You have now bound off one stitch.

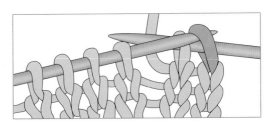

Step 2: Knit the next stitch on the left needle, then insert left needle into the one stitch that remains on the right needle, and draw it over the new stitch and off the needle. You have bound off another stitch.

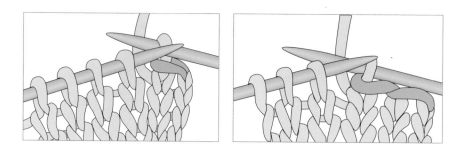

When you have bound off all of your remaining stitches, there will be one stitch left on the right needle. To finish off the yarn, cut the yarn from the ball, leaving about a 4" yarn end. With the right needle, draw this end up and through the last stitch.

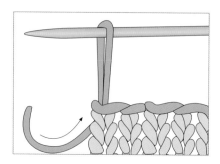

SEWING SEAMS

Usually the pattern you are working on will tell you which type of seam to make. Use the same yarn you used in the project to sew the seams unless the yarn is too thick. In that case, use a thinner yarn in the same color.

If you have no other instructions, here is a simple seam that can be used for many projects.

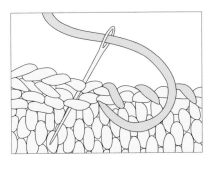

Cut an 18" piece of matching yarn and thread it into the yarn needle. With the right sides of the pieces facing each other and the stitches placed even in a row, insert the needle from back to front through the strands at the edges of the pieces between the stitches. Pull the yarn end gently but firmly. The two pieces will come together. Weave in all loose yarn ends.

Here is another seam which is very useful for joining two edges together, as in the hat on page 64. Sew the edges together working one stitch from each side. Weave in all loose ends.

WEAVING IN THE ENDS

   When you have completed all of your knitting, you will find yarn ends including the ones left at the beginning of the cast on row, as well as the yarn end from your binding off.

   Thread the ends in a yarn needle (a needle with a large eye and a blunt tip) and weave it through the backs of your stitches. Weave about 2" in one direction and then about 1" in the opposite direction. Trim off any extra yarn.

   Never allow your yarn needle to go through to the front of the project.

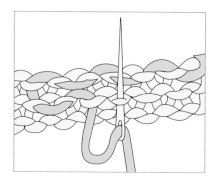

Index

Standard Yarn Weights

To make it easier for yarn manufacturers, publishers and designer to prepare consumer-friendly products and for consumers to select the right materials for a project, the following standard yarn weight system has been adopted.

Yarn Weight Symbol & Names	SUPER FINE 1	FINE 2	LIGHT 3	MEDIUM 4	BULKY 5	SUPER BULKY 6
Type of Yarns in Category	Sock, Fingering, Baby	Sport, Baby	DK, Light Worsted	Worsted, Afghan, Aran	Chunky, Craft, Rug	Bulky, Roving
Knit Gauge Range* in Stockinette St to 4" (10 cm)	27-32 sts	23-26 sts	21-24 sts	16-20 sts	12-15 sts	6-11 sts
Advised Needle Size Range	1 to 3	3 to 5	5 to 7	7 to 9	9 to 11	11 and larger

*GUIDELINES ONLY: The chart above reflects the most commonly used gauges and needle sizes for specific yarn categories.